By Michael Sandler
Illustrated by Ron Mahoney

Scott Foresman
is an imprint of

Glenview, Illinois • Boston, Massachusetts • Chandler, Arizona •
Upper Saddle River, New Jersey

Illustrations
Ron Mahoney.

ISBN 13: 978-0-328-51399-4
ISBN 10   0-328-51399-7

6 7 8 9 10 V0FL 16 15 14 13

I'd been on the driveway practicing for hours.

Then, I realized I wasn't alone. My little sister, Shona, was watching me from the side of the garage.

"What do you call that, Asha?" she asked loudly. She did everything loudly.

I dropped my basketball. "You weren't supposed to be watching," I said. "Nobody was. If you need to know, Shona, it's my reverse triple fake fadeaway scoop shot. Please, Shona, don't tell anyone about it."

Everyone on the fourth grade basketball team is really good—except me. I'm just average. I'm not tall. I'm not fast. I'm not a good guard, but I love basketball. I think about it day and night. It's like a disease. Now I'm working on my own special shot. I call it the *r-t-f-f-s-s*. I haven't yet shown it to anyone, and I wasn't going to until it's perfect.

I picked up the ball again. I freeze and spin one way and then the other way. Then, falling backwards, I scoop the ball up toward the hoop. The ball rolls around the rim and drops through the net. I do this over and over again.

"Yes!!!" I said proudly.

"Asha?" my father shouted, his voice coming from inside the house. "Where are you? Don't forget that we've got to go soon."

I'd been so busy working on my *r-t-f-f-s-s*, I'd almost forgotten. Today, the three of us were going to take a trip to the Basketball Hall of Fame. It would only take an hour or two to get there.

"I haven't forgotten," I said as I raced inside.

Ten minutes later, our car was already stuck in a knot of traffic. Shona sat next to me chewing on a granola bar. She was making crunching noises, loud ones. I ignored them and continued to study the article that Dad had printed out: "A Guide to the Naismith Memorial Basketball Hall of Fame."

"Dad," I asked, "why is the Hall in Springfield? Why isn't it in a really big city like New York or Boston or Chicago?"

"Ah," he replied, "that's because Springfield is important to basketball. Basketball was invented in Springfield."

"Why did they name it the Naismith Hall of Fame? Naismith is not an easy word to say," I wondered out loud.

"James Naismith invented the sport back in 1891," Dad answered.

Suddenly, Shona decided to pay attention to something besides her granola bar. "What's a hall of fame?" she asked.

"It's a museum—this one's for sports," I said. "It honors the best players and coaches in basketball."

"Ohhhh," Shona said as she yawned and looked out the window.

When we finally rolled into the parking lot, I was surprised. The building looked like nothing I had ever seen. It was shaped like a giant silver basketball!

The inside of the Hall of Fame was equally remarkable. There was a full-sized basketball court and walls lined with photos.

"Wow, look how many photos there are," I said.

"You know," said Dad, "basketball is one of the most popular sports in the world. Millions of people play the game, so two hundred photos on these walls isn't really that many. You must be a very special player to have your picture here. You must be voted in. You must be the best of the best."

We moved through the halls, stopping to look at display cases filled with uniforms, shoes, trophies, and newspaper articles written about basketball players.

Then we saw a basketball on display. It was Wilt Chamberlain's! He used this very one to score his 25,000th point.

"His 25,000th point," I said. "Amazing!"

"Nobody scored like Wilt," said Dad. "Nobody. He once scored a hundred points in a game. In the fifty years since, no one has done it again. And Wilt was one of the first really, really big guys—more than seven feet tall."

Wilt Chamberlain

Farther on were two life-sized models. One was so tall that he looked like a human skyscraper.

"Who's this?" I asked, standing next to the tall one. I didn't even reach his waist.

"The tallest NBA player ever," said Dad. "Manute Bol."

"He was really this tall?" asked Shona, staring up at Manute's face.

"Yup," said Dad, "just a few inches short of eight feet."

We turned to the other player. He wasn't tall. In fact, he was shorter than Dad.

"This is Muggsy Bogues—the shortest player in NBA history," said Dad. "Muggsy was fast as lightning. Muggsy could run rings around everybody else. You know you don't have to be the tallest. You just need to have something special that you call your own."

Down the hall, Shona was trying to sound out a name on a display. "Lay-dee," she said.

"It's Lad-dee," Dad said. "Laddie Gale was one of the first players to shoot with one hand. In the old days, everyone used two hands."

I thought about my special shot, the *r-t-f-f-s-s*. Nobody was doing it now. Maybe someday everybody would.

"Don't they have any lay-dees here?" said Shona, giggling at her joke.

"Absolutely," said Dad. "Look."

"Burr-thay," read Shona.

"Bertha," helped Dad. "Bertha Teague was a high school coach in Oklahoma. Her teams almost never lost. At one point, they won 98 straight games."

Dad pointed to a different display. "That's Nancy Lieberman. She won college championships and played in the Olympics. She was also the first female ever to play in a men's pro league. They called her 'Lady Magic.'"

I liked the sound of that name.

Nancy Lieberman

Downstairs we saw another Magic—Magic Johnson. He was up on a video screen. He was so graceful and elegant as he flashed through the air and slammed the ball through the hoop. It was amazing to watch him in action.

"He looks like he's seven feet tall!" said Shona.

"Not quite, but he played like he was," Dad replied. "Magic could guard players of any size. That's one of the things that made him so special."

Magic Johnson

Heading downstairs, we saw a James Naismith statue.

"Why's he holding a trash bin?" asked Shona.

"It's not a trash bin," said Dad, smiling. "It's a wooden basket—a peach basket. That was what he used as a net for the very first game." Wow. All I could think was how glad I was that he had such a special mind to think up such a great game.

Finally, we reached the basketball court. There was a section with shorter baskets, perfect for little kids.

I passed Shona a ball, and she tossed it up toward the net.

"This is fun," she said softly.

I realized that I'd enjoyed being with my sister today.

"Asha, why don't you show Dad your special move?" Shona said, almost in a whisper.

At first I was really, really angry. Why couldn't she keep a secret? But then Dad said he really wanted to see whatever it was that I could do. Maybe now *was* the right time to show off my new move.

Dad watched carefully as I dribbled. Then I spun, faked, scooped, and performed my *r-t-f-f-s-s*. The ball sank smoothly into the net.

Dad applauded. So did some other people who had gathered nearby to watch.

"Wow, one day that shot could land *you* in the Hall of Fame," Dad said proudly.

"That's what I was thinking too," Shona added.

Maybe, I thought to myself, just maybe they were right! Today, I'd learned some things about myself. There are many ways we can each be special.

James Naismith

James Naismith was a YMCA gym teacher in Springfield, Massachusetts, when he invented the game of basketball. During cold winters, when the grounds outside the YMCA froze, students had to stay indoors. To keep them busy and happy, in 1891 Naismith invented a game that could be played inside a gym.

The Naismith Memorial Basketball Hall of Fame opened in Springfield in 1968. It honors the game's inventor as well as the players and coaches who have helped to build the sport. As of 2008, 258 people have been voted into basketball's Hall of Fame.

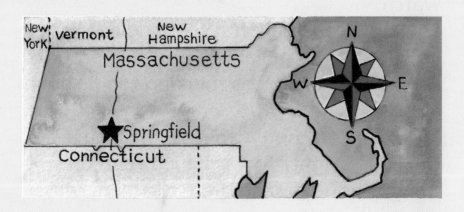